THE BRIGHTEST DARK

Poems from an obsessed, anxious
and depressed mind

C. H. Lakes

Copyright © 2022 C. H. Lakes

All rights reserved

No part of this book may be reproduced, or stored in a retrieval system, or transmitted in any form or by any means, electronic, mechanical, photocopying, recording, or otherwise, without express written permission of the publisher.

To everyone out there who is struggling with mental illnesses. It's not your fault, and you shouldn't be embarrassed or afraid of talking about it. This is just as important as any physical illness. I know it can get very hard because sometimes, those around you don't have the tools or knowledge to understand you. I know it can get terribly lonely and painful. But I published this book FOR YOU. Because I care about you. Because I hope that at least one line in this book makes you see that someone else understands exactly how you feel. You're not alone. Don't give up. You can feel better. I believe in you.

To anyone who wants to gain some insight into how someone with mental health issues can feel. Thank you for caring about this subject. I hope this helps you help others.

To A. L. who unknowingly encouraged me to keep writing after her unexpectedly positive reaction to the first poem in this book. This probably wouldn't exist without you.

To those who encouraged me to make this public through their amazing feedback.

CONTENTS

Title Page
Copyright
Dedication
Preface
Maze   1
Small-town Clown   3
The Great Alarm   4
What Would I Write   5
Maze 2   6
The Prairie   10
Functional Dysfunctional   12
Would You   13
Fade   14
Dripping   15
Wish   16
I Dream   17
The-ra-py   19
The Prank   21
Speak   22
The Speech Machine   23
Run   24

Maybe It Was	25
Out Of Place	26
Can't Even	27
A Cold Shower	28
I'm So	29
Take You To Places	30
The Tree	32
Neglection	33
Falling	34
Hands	36
Isn't It Both Awful And Romantic	37
Tiny Velvet Box	39
Soap Bubbles	40
The Act	41
Twelve Hours	43
Room Full Of Mirrors	44
Before I Say Goodbye	46
About To Rain	48
Something That I Can Hold On To	49
The Thing	51
Yesterday's Special	52
Shadows	53
Spaces	54
A Chance	56
Pupils	57
Planet	59
Mis Pasos	61
¿Quiénes Somos?	62

Pierdo Mi Aliento	63
Colgando En El Viento	65
Lastre	67
Invisible	68
Fantasía	70
Correr, Cortar, Romper	72
Thank you	73

PREFACE

A little over a decade ago, around 14 years to be more precise, I was 18 years old. I had been writing poems for a couple of years, but at that time, I was on the brink of being done with writing for good. Writing was a good way of creating something decent whenever ugly thoughts or feelings appeared. It felt good to paint a picture with words. And it felt a little bit better when I found that I had managed to come up with a metaphor that I really liked or with a couple of lines that went particularly well together. So why would I stop doing something that I was apparently enjoying?

Well… The thing is that I was going through very difficult mental health issues at that time. Very few people knew about it. Almost two years had passed since I had been diagnosed with a very severe case of obsessive-compulsive disorder combined with generalized anxiety disorder, something for which I was being treated by a professional. But inevitably for me, everything that I wrote usually reflected that state of mind. My words were frequently filled with angst and despair or deep sadness. Even the occasional more optimistic poem was still surrounded by this heavy, gray haze. And I couldn't handle that. I couldn't tolerate the fact that those words that didn't sound happy were coming from me. I couldn't accept the fact that those dark feelings and thoughts were part of me. I was scared of them. There was only one "normal" and "correct" state of mind to me back then, and that was happiness. So if these were definitely not happy words, then it had to mean that something was wrong with me; I could even be going crazy. I thought that everything that I was writing was wrong and unacceptable. I was embarrassed. Yet somewhere along the way, I found the courage to show what I had been writing to a couple of select close friends. I don't know exactly why I did it, maybe to get some of it out of my system, but to my surprise, they liked it. I didn't understand how that could be. The idea of those words resulting in something that seemed to possess some kind of beauty in the eyes of others was something that I simply couldn't come to terms with. I found it terribly messed up, and I definitely didn't want to have anything to do with it. Emotional pain, sadness, anxiety and despair going hand in hand with beauty? I just couldn't wrap my head around it. It all seemed so wrong to me, and the more I thought about it, the more I wanted to run away from it, the more it made me sick, the more I wanted to sweep it under the carpet and never have to look at it again. And eventually, I just stopped.

I stopped writing altogether for about 14 years. I was terrified of it. The year I turned 19, every notebook containing my writings had already been hidden in a dark corner of my room. And life went on. I got over my mental health crisis, stopped any sort of therapy sessions and got off my meds; but soon enough, things started to get bad again. I started having more and more obsessions that made me increasingly anxious. But I had such bad memories from my previous crisis, and I was so anxious, that the sole idea of going back to seek professional help made me fear that they wouldn't understand me, that their words would only mess up my head even more. So it took me several years of additional tortuous episodes to actually have the guts to start going to therapy with a psychologist again.

One day after I had been listening to some sad music that was in line with my state of mind, and after a couple of therapy sessions had already gone by, some words started gathering in my head. They definitely weren't happy words. But I just had to write them down because they just kept coming in. I couldn't stop my brain from generating words and lines, and I had to dump them somewhere. So I did it. I wrote.

In an attempt to better express how I was feeling to my therapist – much to my embarrassment – I made a bold move and shared my Frankenstein with them. And, man, was I in for a shock... This person told me that my poem had actually made them tear up. Later, when we spoke more about it, they told me that it was "beautiful". I was very confused. Again... "Beautiful"??? How could such dark words that talked about emotional pain and utter despair create something beautiful and not something that was inherently unpleasant, wrong and sick??? It felt like my brain wanted to throw up... But my therapist continued and told me that it was like what happened with songs. Some songs have lyrics that talk about very emotionally painful situations. They're even accompanied by melodies that also sound very sad and heavy. And yet if that pain is described using subtle imagery combined with those words that feel just right and with fitting music, the kind that manages to pull at your heart strings, you find yourself immersed in a bittersweet experience that can in the end only be described as "beautiful". Although that doesn't take away the painful part from it, a sort of work of art is created. And those words kind of started to turn things around in my head... And the conversation kept going. We talked about how we shouldn't be ashamed of not feeling great, of feeling scared, anxious, sad, or of having ideas pop up in our heads with which we might not agree.

We're so used to going to the doctor when we have a cold or a fever or are in physical pain. We listen to them, we take our medication and we might even have to skip work or school for a couple of days. We rest. We go to the dentist if we have a bad tooth ache. We go to the ER if we just had an accident. We talk to our friends about how painful that dental procedure was, or about how it still hurts when we bite something too hard. We even ask others for help.

But telling someone that you haven't been feeling very optimistic lately, that you're rather down, that each day is starting to feel harder to live than the other, that you don't really know why, but you're starting to wonder if you should even be alive? Or telling your boss that you were too anxious to concentrate the week before and that that's the reason why you weren't able to finish your work on time? Or telling your friends that you took longer than normal in the bathroom because you were having an anxiety attack and you were trying to calm yourself down? Oh, no. No one wants to do any of that. Why? Because we're afraid of others not understanding, of them calling us "crazy" or "exaggerated", of our situations being belittled or trivialized. And sadly, this can be the case with some people. Although progress has been made, mental health is still a stigmatized subject, and more among some age groups or in some countries, for example, than in others. To many, only "crazy" people go to a therapist or need to take medication.

All this is very dangerous. Take for example a person who is feeling deeply sad but who doesn't even understand why, or who can't face or handle the reason behind their extreme sadness, or a person who is completely exhausted of living a life in which everything feels like a threat, or in which any subject can turn into unwanted thoughts or images that never stop spinning in their minds. If this person doesn't feel safe enough to talk about their situation with someone else, things will keep getting harder for them. What if they're already thinking of negative ways in which they can completely stop or at least diminish their pain and nobody knows about it? These persons' state is so fragile that they won't have the strength to go looking around trying to find someone who doesn't judge them. It's very easy for a person in these conditions to commit suicide. And the world will have lost someone who didn't get to live the best life that they could, or to give back all that they could have.

These hypothetical persons that we've been talking about are real, and they're out there. And their state is too weak to convince others of their situation being valid and an urgent matter. It's up to everyone else, to all those who have at least a bit of strength in them, to show people around them that they won't judge them, that they're available to listen and care and help.

Being deeply sad, extremely worried or frightened, having excessively intrusive thoughts, images, or sensations harassing you, or feeling the urge to do certain actions in a certain way in an attempt to avoid something seemingly terrible from happening is not an exaggerated behavior that a person chooses to act out. These are all mental illnesses that are eventually also related to a person's brain chemistry: depression, anxiety disorders, panic disorders and obsessive-compulsive disorder are all prime examples. People diagnosed with mental health conditions aren't making it up. They aren't faking it or choosing to act that way. They aren't crazy either. They are very aware of what they're going through and of the pain that it's causing them. They have an illness that they can't stop or make go away. What they can and should do is seek professional help. This includes therapy and medication if necessary. Both of these will help people learn how to handle their situation better and live the best life that they can. But they will have a harder time finding the strength to do them if they don't have someone close that's supporting them.

It might not be as normal to suffer from mental health issues as having a cold is, but it certainly should be as normal to talk about them as it is about any physical illnesses. Mental illnesses are just as important as physical illnesses, and they should be treated with the same amount of respect, compassion, professionalism and urgency.

As I said before, it's up to everyone who has even a little bit of strength in them to take part in creating a society in which talking about your mental health is normal and not stigmatized. You might not notice it right away, but you will be literally contributing to saving lives. This responsibility of contributing to the removal of the stigma around mental health is especially important if you're going through mental health issues yourself, because you have first-hand experience that can more easily help others. So let me start:

I'm C. H. Lakes, a woman born exactly in 1990 who lives in Latin America. My real story with mental health started when I was around 15 years old. I've been diagnosed with disorders related to OCD, anxiety and depression. For a very long time, I felt like it was somehow wrong, as well as unpleasant for others, to talk about the feelings and experiences related to these mental illnesses. Because of this, I completely stopped writing for around 14 years, an activity that I was actually starting to enjoy back when I started it at 16, but that inevitably made me talk about my unhappy feelings and experiences. I've spent a big chunk of my life hating the different jobs that I've had and looking for a financially productive activity that I could also actually enjoy. When I finally had the guts to seek professional help again, I was eventually able to understand that it's not my fault to have these mental health issues, that it's not something that I'm choosing to do, that I'm not doing anything wrong or choosing to behave or react in the ways caused by my disorders. These are illnesses just like any other, and therefore, there should be nothing wrong in talking about how it feels to have them. Thanks to that, I started writing again, and I even took the plunge and am publishing my first book of poems about mental health! I was advised by my therapist to get a doctor's opinion on whether I should take medication to help with my symptoms. It took some trial and error, but when you find the right medication and dosages, it really makes a difference in due time. I'm still very much in the beginning of my journey towards accepting my situation and towards learning how to handle my different mental health problems, but if you're suffering from mental health issues, I can only tell you that you have to give yourself a chance. Don't give up! Go look for professional help. You CAN feel better! Don't lose hope! You're NOT trapped. This is NOT the end. There's PLENTY of mental health professionals out there, and I bet that they will be more than pleased to help you. Give them a chance too. Try your best to be completely honest with them from the start. Try to be consistent, to be patient, to be kind and loving to yourself, and also, don't let your fear of facing your mental health issues get in the way of you living the best life you could live!

I'd love to hear your story. Let's connect on Instagram (c.h.lakes); you can also use the hashtag #MyMentalHealthMatters to share your story with others too.

I hope you can find some comfort, solace, courage or understanding of others' situations in these words that you're about to read. Oh, and also perhaps some beauty. The beauty found when you intertwine the dark fibers of reality in a way that makes them shimmer under the sun, creating a sort of shiny darkness; so if you get the darkest fibers and weave them together, you might just end up creating the brightest dark.

MAZE

I'm sitting in a maze
I'm staring in a daze
Trying to push out these walls
I just can't seem to feel okay

I'm starstruck, hypnotized
By all the voices that can't leave my mind

I still see your eyes
Yeah, I can still hear your voice
I can still hear me cry
While I'm desperate to run and hide

It's like an airplane crashing and burning
Like a fire thriving with power

You see the smoke
You hear the screaming
You stretch your hand out
No one's leaning

And time just stood still
But time won't stop going by
I can hear the ticking and creaking
While the voices just keep bickering

Is the air thinner here?
Is the night darker tonight?
Am I still up for a fight?
Will I ever just see some light?

But the lights are on
And the lights are off
And I'm up and down
And I'm all around

When will all this end?
I can see no friends
I can't see my face
Hidden in the maze

Where it all began
Where you see no end
Locked up in pretend
Wrapped up in these chains

SMALL-TOWN CLOWN

In the smallest of towns
In the darkest of places
There once was a clown
Who loved to switch faces

The Monday face was sunny
The Tuesday face was bright
The Wednesday face was rocky
And the Thursday one a bit dry

When Friday came, he looked sloppy
By Saturday night he was sad
Then Sunday all day
He went out of his way
To look a little less mad

The next day would come
And the whole town would yawn
The clown would get up
And the gears would snap

Right into place
To build a new face
Start a new day
With all in his way

THE GREAT ALARM

Stare right into the night
When your feet feel cold
As they brush the ground

Save space as you lift your arms
To make way for the great alarm
It will take everything you've got
To stay safe from the big attack

Just pray that you can come back
From the place where it all goes black
Just stay for a little longer
Don't cave; I begin to wonder

If this is it
If that's that
I'm out of it
Am I a fit?

Am I here?
Am I there?
I'm everywhere
But I'm nowhere

WHAT WOULD I WRITE

So what would I write
If everything was right
And nothing was wrong?
Would I sing a song?

Of sorrow and pain
Until I could faint?
Of giants and mice?
Would I throw the dice?

Would I gamble with fate?
Give up on this race?
Open the door?
Scream at the floor?

Would I tell a story
Of lost faded glory?
Of mighty old dreams?
And eloquent trees?

Would I fall apart?
Would you play the part?
Would you act like you care?
Or would you stop and stare?

MAZE 2

It's dark
It's cold
It's heavy
There's mold

No air
No space
In a daze
It's a maze

I look back
Look down
To the sides
I push around

Try to find
A way out
Of this drought
I'm so not fine

This place
Is no maze
It's here
The real deal

It's a blaze
It's a knife
It's a grave
It's cyanide

Count one

Count two
Count three
Set me free

Count four
Count five
Count six
Let me be

'Cause this place
Is no maze
It's here
The real deal

How did I
Get this far?
When did I
Fall apart?

I'm trying
To stand up
But my knees
Are so weak

I'm trying
To move my mouth
But it seems
Like all's gone south

My voice
Won't come out
The noise
Won't shut up

My lungs
Will just die
Without air
Full despair

My ears
Will explode
It's so loud
I want out

My eyes
Just can't see
What's right in
Front of me

My hands
Can't seem to touch
What I fear
I might've lost

I'm blind
I'm deaf
I'm cold
In this hole

In this cardboard maze
This abandoned cage
Where the sun doesn't shine
And the air won't blow

Where despair
Is the heir
Of all precious
Possessions

You can't run
You can't hide
Gotta hold on
Too tight

While the fire
Sears your face
While you lose

Your own name

Your reflection
Will fade
You'll be lost
In a place

That's so big
Yet so small
And so cold
And so dark

In this huge
Cardboard box
Where the giants
Squash mice

Where the cries
For what's lost
Are the song
Of the frost

In this place
That's no maze
'Cause it's real
And it's here

It's so loud
In this cage
And it's real
And it's here

THE PRAIRIE

Remember when we laughed?
When we played all day?
I loved seeing your smile
Even for just a little while

I loved how the wind
Played with your hair
It was so unfair
But I couldn't help but stare

And when we heard that song
For the first time
The tears built up in your eyes
It felt like nothing could go wrong

With your snowy skin
And velvet voice
You grabbed me by the wrist
And pushed out the noise

You led me through the storm
Through the fierce fire
You looked me in the eye
When all was dire

We arrived in a magical place
Where it never got late
Where flowers would sing
And you'd float but never sink

It was this gorgeous prairie

Brimming with daisies
Gushing and rushing
With rivers aplenty

And the air was so light
You could feel yourself floating
And the breeze tasted sweet
All the torches were glowing

But the dark hits the light
Every once in a while
You stop dead in your tracks
As you hear yourself crack

Crack the rock; grab my hand
Sail away in the sand
As we blast through the past
And find freedom at last

FUNCTIONAL DYSFUNCTIONAL

Do you even know what I mean?
When dysfunctional meets functional
When barely functioning isn't even functioning
When trying doesn't cut it

The transgression of this progression
Is just aggression to my possessions
And the end seems near
And the end seems here

What a fault, what a foul
Who's to blame for this mess?
Wanna throw in the towel
To the rising distress

The high water keeps rushing
And the walls just keep crumbling
I hear the sound of the crushing
And the silence approaching

WOULD YOU

If I paint a picture of your face
Would you swear you'd stay?
If I flip the switch and take a hit
Would you love me a little bit?

If I take the leap across this strait
Would it make you wait?
If I wipe the tears off my face
Would it set things straight?

'Cause the scars that I carry
Are the way to my soul
But the hands that I bury
Are the doom of us both

And the longer you look
The less you will find
The deeper the book
The darker the grind

FADE

I could drown in the darkness
Be swallowed by the noise
I could sink in the blindness
Until I lost my voice

I could fade in the mist
I could float away
Wrapped in a lullaby
Of silences that lost their way

And the shadows would hug me
The frost would embrace me
The echoes would listen
Under endless waves of slumber

DRIPPING

So the water won't stop dripping
I thought I'd really fixed it
But all I see is holes
I might just end up tripping

I guess I'm bad at figuring out
The simple things in life
I'm tired of this drought
But the water won't stop dripping

And now I'm getting itchy
This mess is making me nervous
Where will I get a new hose
Like the one I had before?

But the water won't stop dripping
Now the floor looks like a pool
A mop will be no good
I might just end up falling

Who do you call
Before you fall
Before you trip
'Cause the water won't stop dripping?

WISH

I wish I could break free
Move my feet across the lake
Fill my lungs with air
Stride without fear or being scared

I wish I could meet you there
Touch your face, smell your hair
Breathe you in
I think we could win

I wish you could be my saving grace
The night's first star
Shining brightly from start to end
Without leaving a scar

I wish I could take you everywhere
I know you'd tag along no matter where
And if someone dared to stop and stare
we'd walk away without being scared

We'd walk in the light
Of a thousand suns
Blinded by their bright eyes
But we'd be home

I DREAM

I dreamt I could find you
In the depths of this mansion
I walked across the corridors
Stepped on some old photos

There were thousands of them
Some were old and washed out
Others new but grayed out
But they all reminded me of back then

Back then when you lived in this mansion
You had your own room, your own covers
You left your stuff all over
This was your place, no question

Your freckles glittered in the sunlight
The sunbeams went right into your bright eyes
Rosy apples danced on your cheeks
I could take in that light show all week

But then I woke up with a scare
As I saw it was actually me who'd lost the key
I couldn't understand; I couldn't dare
I couldn't see how the one left outside was me

I couldn't believe it was me who'd lost my key
I started looking for it in a frenzy
I thought about how you'd get lonely in the mansion
I had to be there, no question

I searched and searched to no avail

Suddenly I felt like I was in jail
Locked outside of my own mansion
I was starting to feel the tension

Locked outside of my own house
Knowing that you were inside?
I knocked and knocked
Until my skin cracked

But you couldn't hear me
And I couldn't get in
How did this happen?
How did I lose my own key?

And now I'm left outside in the cold
Looking at these photos that are getting old
Finding you in my dreams
While in reality I can only scream

THE-RA-PY

I'm having a hard time trusting you
Would you mind if I admit that I do?
All the lines and circles become blurry
I don't know, but this shit's becoming scary

I try to focus on your face
But suddenly I'm captured in a daze
I can't keep up with the pace
We should really continue this another day

But I gotta keep pushing
Don't mind if I'm bruising
Who cares if I'm abusing
Your time and my mind

But I'm losing your voice
And I'm losing my voice
I can't keep out the noise
Am I just a toy?

Without a say
Without power
Not here to stay
Just a flower?

And I'm having a hard time believing you
Are you here to stay or will you crush me too?
What would you say if I asked you to care?
Would that be a burden? Would you call me rare?

I don't wanna beg

But I'll beg
Just tell me you won't stare
Promise me you'll care

Please just break the silence
Please bring in some noise
Please raise your soft voice
Please, just please, don't be a toy

THE PRANK

So I played guitar for an hour
I'd love to tell you I showered
But we both know I'd be lying
I'm kind of tired of trying

I went back to bed with the hope
That it would rain all day nonstop
But I didn't even see one drop
I was staring lifeless feeling like a prop

I told myself I'd try to take a nap
But like a slap on the face, I saw it was a trap
Suddenly I found myself not being able to escape
The sights and sounds I thought belonged to yesterday

With nowhere to go, nowhere to run
I leapt out of bed, walked down the stairs
I sat on that chair, gasped for some air
Got sucked into the void of empty words

And as the dark settled, I filled up a kettle
Of bittersweet tea and lost melodies
I stretched out the blankets, got stuck in a blank
Then I wondered and pondered: Was this all just a prank?

SPEAK

I must've read that email a thousand times
I would find something wrong in every single line
I just couldn't find the words to express
The level I had reached with this whole mess

How do you go from silence to noise
When the noise has gone out of bounds?
How do you turn thoughts into sound?
How do you make a broken ballerina go round?

It's like I have to fight a beast
I have to swim against the current
I can't handle this endless torrent
I might just drown under this torment

I try to catch some air as you stare
I try to lift the blocks, build a house
But I'm feeling trapped like a mouse
It's not fair; I look like I'm not there, but I care

THE SPEECH MACHINE

I think I might've fractured
A piece of this contraption
I just can't find some traction
The light or its refraction

I can't give you a reaction
I just can't spring into action
The cogs are filled with rust
This machine's turning into dust

And this factory is crumbling
I'm trapped inside; I'm stumbling
Can't see the light; I'm fumbling
Can't hear my voice; it's rumbling

The closer I get to the door
The more cracks appear on the floor
I really want there to be more
Please just help me open the door

RUN

I really just wanna run away, go home
Hide away and cry away
Until I can get the poison out of my bones

I wish I could tell you I wanna stay
But the glint in my eyes would say otherwise
I wish I didn't have to stay here for another day

I wanna go home, but where's home?
What's home when every place feels like a dark maze?
All the walls are cold, and you get scraped by the stone

Where do you go? Where do you hide?
I'm running all day waiting for some rain
I'm waiting all the time to be able to escape

I see the sunlight, but I want it to be nighttime
I see the night, how it blinds
I see the darkness, how it tosses and turns
I feel the walls, how they sting and burn

I want to escape; not sure I should stay
The shadows are haunting; this all seems so daunting
But this is what's real; this is what's true; I just have to see it through
And the river's music numbs me; I try to repeat this the whole week
I just hope it doesn't get too steep

MAYBE IT WAS

I wanted to write something to help me feel better
But the words just won't come out; maybe it's this weather
Maybe it was this day with its haze
Or this week that was so steep
Or this month with its maze

Whatever the cause
It all seems like a fuzz
I wish I could pause
This inevitable rush

I wanted to write something to help me feel bigger
But when the words come out, I get smaller
Maybe it was yesterday's night that got so dark
Or the week before, how it tore
Or last month with its marks

Whatever the cause
I can't seem to touch the ground
I just want to come around
And stop watching the sun go down

OUT OF PLACE

Like a zebra with red stripes
Like the sun in the middle of the night
Like rain dripping upwards
Like Snow White without her dwarfs

You're out of place
You're not from around
You can't show your face
You might hit the ground

Like a black sky in the afternoon
Like a blunt knife and a flat spoon
Like a silent song filling the room
Like a summer breeze that's about to freeze

You don't belong
You can't find your way
You're trapped in this day
Like a never-ending song

CAN'T EVEN

Lately I can't even write
I don't even know if I'm right
I can't tell if these things are real
It all seems like an ordeal

I try to get up
But I get pulled to the ground
I try to open my eyes
But all I see is ice

I try to open the door
But it doesn't even have a knob
I try to break the walls
But I end up dancing a waltz

I try to remember
But my head is just embers
Don't wanna give in
But it's pulling me in

My stomach's a rock
I wanna throw up
Throw me a bone
Help me go home

A COLD SHOWER

I don't even know who I miss
Who this person is
I try to turn around and twist
But she keeps grabbing me by the wrist

I ask, "how did you get here?"
She says, "I've always been here"
"It's you who's wanted to stay clear"
I look away in fear

I try to deny these lies
I try to close my eyes
And like a cold shower
It all hits me with so much power

I see she's right
I look at her with pleading eyes
I tell her, "please, let's just escape"
"Let's get away before it's too late"

The sadness builds up in her eyes
I think she's gonna cry
As she tells me that we have to stay
We have to do this for another day
If we don't, we might both die
I realize she's right, so I cry

I'M SO

And I'm so sad in a way that freezes me
Not in a way that moves me
Would you move me?

And I'm so tired I can see the lines deepen
All I see is circles and shapes lost in the haze
Shadows and fractions that I'm trying to capture
Figures and numbers and sounds that just keep moving the ground

Will everything stop spinning if I stay still?
I wish I had a drill so I could break the ground
Break the glass, break the walls; see it all fall

I wish this was all an illusion not this intrusion
There's so much confusion, but it's just an illusion
It's not real; it's not here

It's unreal how close everything feels
It's like you're captured while being fractured
And suddenly you're away in another space
It's another time; it's another day

It's like a black hole that sucks you in
It swallows you whole; you can't win
It transports you; it transforms you
Who will I be when I find myself free?

TAKE YOU TO PLACES

It's crazy how I can take you to places
You didn't even imagine
Just take my hand
You'll see we're closer than we're apart

Just jump right in
Give yourself a chance to win
Dive into my eyes
Let me take you on a flight

I'll make you soar through blue skies
You'll feel the air brushing your hair
You'll feel the breeze tickling your face
You'll realize this is a paradise

Breathe in the sunlight
Let it turn your soul bright
Let yourself be blinded by the dark
As it shines through the black night

Let your voice melt into the choir
Of a thousand brilliant sounds
As you let yourself spin round
And twirl to your heart's desire

Shut the noise; dive deep
Put the water through your feet
Swim and leap among the colors
Color your feathers to this weather

It's crazy how I can take you to places

You didn't even imagine
Just take my hand
You'll see we're closer than we're apart

THE TREE

Please don't tell me lies
Please don't even try
Try to understand
That unless you take my hand
I won't be able to stand

And I wish I could stand this
I wish I could stand us
I wish I could stand me
I wish I could break free
Climb high into that tree
As I watch everything turn to dust
Turn to ashes
The floor crumbling; the ceiling rumbling

And the water's coming
The river's rushing
I can feel the cold in my toes
I sprint and run; I just have to go
Don't wanna get caught in the current
The water's whispers sound too urgent

I jump and fall from the tree
I stumble and scrape my knee
It stings, but I can still see
And like lightning I spring away
And escape from this dreadful fate

NEGLECTION

I had neglected neglection
I didn't realize the size
Of the lack of affection
Correction:
I hadn't realized the depth of the hole
Now I'm trapped like a mole

Blindsided by the light
Don't even know what's right
I wanna give up
But I stay for the fight
But all I feel is the cold
I'm trapped like a mole

I try to feel my way
Out of this place
But every turn I take
I hit another wall
I'm trapped like a mole

I think I just need a break
Maybe I can stay awake
If not, who will take my place?

FALLING

I can see the strands of your hair
Floating upwards in the air
Moving like they cared
Like they don't want to be there

And I can see your eyes
Staring blankly into the sky
I can see the helplessness in their voice
Like they didn't have a choice

I can see your mouth
It's frozen throughout
Your lips glisten with white sparkles
Your expression as cold as marbles

And I can see your arms
As they desperately try to hold on to something
They move with alarm
Until they just don't move any longer
And give in to the fall

When did you start to fall?
It feels like a second frozen in time
Yet time never stopped going by
And you continue to endlessly fall

The speed of the wind is making you deaf
The scrape of the air is cutting your skin
This inhuman breeze is making your eyes sting
This violent current stripped off all your clothes

At the beginning you float; you glide
Then you start to stumble and dive
You're diving fast; you're falling
You try to stop, but you keep falling

HANDS

I could stare at my hands all day
Wondering where they've been, where they've hidden, what they've done
Tracing each curve, each turn, each crease
I wonder what I'll find, maybe some dirt? Some grease?

I turn them around while I try to think
And figure out where that tiny scar came from
Was it in April? Was it in March? Was I being strong?
Or maybe I was being weak and naive and slipped and hit a sink?

It doesn't matter what I think or what I remember
These hands tell their own story
It doesn't matter if I'm here or already there
The voice of this rough skin will talk without worry

When this voice is dried up and gone
Its echoes will be drowned out by the noises of the voices
Of those who would rather listen to the marks on skins and bones
Than to the truths told by their bearer's voice

ISN'T IT BOTH AWFUL AND ROMANTIC

Isn't it rough?
Isn't it enough?
Won't the passage of time
Make me go blind?
Won't the weight of the air
Make me trip and fall down the stairs?

Isn't it both awful and romantic
How you can't stop chasing me?
You can't stop tasing me?
You immobilize me with your static
It seems to make you ecstatic
I'm not so elated if you ask me

You breathe my air
You steal my stares
You make me freeze
You make me cry
You start a riot
Then make me laugh

The world's on fire
The world's an ice pool
You take me by a fool
You think I'm just a tool
And yet I'm your deepest desire

But you take me and break me

Harass me and blast me
It's not love; it's just an obsession
How many more of these sessions
Will it take you to make me your possession?

Isn't it rough?
Isn't it enough?
Isn't it both awful and romantic
How you can't stop chasing me?
You can't stop tasing me?

TINY VELVET BOX

What would you say if I told you that I want to capture this moment in a tiny box that I can carry with me at all times? A tiny box covered in soft velvet and glitter and magic. A tiny box with a tiny but invisible keyhole that can only be opened with a hair strand of a golden puppy in its prime?

And if you opened this tiny box, a light show would explode in front of your eyes. A light show would show you what you've forgotten. A light show would blind you with colors you didn't even know existed. And not just colors but sounds. Oh, the sounds. The sounds would take you to long-forgotten islands floating above the clouds where birds fly without feathers, and the weather flies like the birds' feathers.

I would hop on a cloud and travel this enchanted land. I would ask you to take my hand and jump with me into this tiny velvet box where everything is possible, and anything is plausible. It's a million nautical miles away from the days of dark, from the times apart. It's this tiny infinite world; you can't explain it with words.

It's just light and color and magic and sound. And the echoes of laughter make my heart sing, my soul soar. It's like a soft roar that slowly lifts me up from the ground like I didn't weigh a pound. I'm suddenly floating and gliding through the notes of this pentagram. I grab myself to each shape just to hear its sound, not because I'm afraid to fall. But would you fall? Would you fall with me into this magical place? Would you take my hand and disappear into this forbidden land?

SOAP BUBBLES

Please don't talk to me
I'm starting to break free
From this cage, from this attire
It's like I'm finally starting to cut the wires

Please don't look at me
Your stare is like a snare
I'm beginning to tear
You just pushed me down the stairs

Please just close the door
I don't wanna hear you anymore
I don't wanna hear me being torn
I just want this silence, nothing more

The sound of the silence protects me
And the dark walls wrap me in a hug
This small corner collects my tears
As I spill to it all my fears

The night is dense and heavy
My thoughts floating in the air like soap bubbles
So bright, so empty, and so fragile
Maybe I should just hide them in the rubble

It's no trouble; I do it all the time
I'll just put them in a rhyme
Let some time go by
So that they become stone in the rubble
Like perfectly frozen soap bubbles

THE ACT

Hide my face
Dye my face
Cry my face
Spray my face
My face

Your face looks into my eyes
With an empty expression
I feel like I'm about to cry
But I stop the progression

My face morphs into an impression
My first act's always the most impressive
You can call this a bit repressive
But I gain protection in quick succession

I'm a shape-shifter, a space master
I will sneak past you without making any noise
I will circumvent your words and dilute your voice
But don't push me too far; let's just go faster

Let's wrap up this circus, this charade
After the first act it gets less impressive
I'm tired of being the main act in this parade
Cut me some slack; let's change the narrative

My primal survival instincts kick in
Reality's fading, my heart's beating faster, but I won't let you win
I manage to crawl through that little hole in the wall
With a shattered sense of protection, a dire need for correction;

I'm feeling so small

TWELVE HOURS

I can't believe that in just twelve hours
I'll be sitting here facing you like a cold shower
I can't believe I can't stop that from happening
I never thought things would get so nerve-racking

And I try to think and put my thoughts together
But the haze is thick; I'm under terrible weather
I try to make things stick without them making me sick
I try to thread the needle, but all I get is a prick

I have no recollection; can't make the connections
I'm dying for some correction
For this train of thought that's headed in no direction

And my brain is like Jell-O
I try to comb it; try to squash it
Try to make some pottery with it
But all I hear is "heck no"

Who can tame this master of disaster
This thief in disguise
Who likes to hide in the night?

Who can blame this master of deceit
Who's quick to jump to his feet
Whenever he's called a counterfeit?

I still can't believe that in less than twelve hours
I'll be sitting here facing you like a cold shower

ROOM FULL OF MIRRORS

I'm exactly the kind of person that I don't want to be. I see you, and I fear you because you're like a mirror that reflects what it's like to be me.

I look at myself in total shock; I fall into despair. I'm so scared of facing what it's like to be me. I try so hard to silently run away and hide form what's inside, from who's inside. I spend my days, my weeks, my months, my years trying to stay away from any triggers or traps that could make my real self snap back. I try to hide in disguise; I try to just float by until I don't even remember who I am inside.

I live my life in ignorance of the landscapes, and lakes, and mountains, and lions, and cubs that run and hide. But at the same time, the faintest glimpse of a pawprint reminds me exactly of what's inside. The softest roar of a lion brings me back to reality with a snap. And I realize that I've been running in circles all along. Through time and space, I sleep and wake; I change my clothes; I change my face. I change the pace. I go back and forth dreaming of reaching something I'd adore. And my hopes become intrusions; they seem so close; they seem so near. The excitement of touching the clouds always ends in a frown. They always escape my grip, and then I finally trip.

I was living a life of dreams and mirages of figures rising when only circles were being carved on the ground. I thought I was following the steps of someone who'd already been crowned. But it turned out that the shoes fit perfectly like in a fairy tale, except this was a scary tale.

We're trapped in this eight-wall room. And the creatures' roars start to echo with a boom. And for the first time, I can't escape. I try to turn away and make my head face the other way. But your voice keeps calling me. And I can't escape. You're a room full of mirrors, and in every single one of them, there's a lion or a cub. And they're all ready to attack. I wish I could fight back. I wish I could escape. But maybe this time, it's time to stay. Just for this one time, maybe I can get out of the parade. Maybe I can look you in the eyes and dive into the great lakes. Maybe you'll see me. Maybe you'll find me. Maybe you'll recognize me in the crowd. Maybe I want to stop living a double life just for this little while.

BEFORE I SAY GOODBYE

I'm talking to you
But I'm really not talking
You think the door is open
But it's actually closed
I don't know when things got broken
I just hit the floor

You want me to start walking
But I can't anymore
At least for now
I'm on a pause
I'm on a break
About to break

Just let me stay a little longer
Let me be away so I can ponder
I wonder how we got this far
I wonder when we fell apart
Is it too late to play our parts
Or is it time to be apart?

I swear I didn't mean to
I give you my word I always tried
I tried to take your hand
I tried to understand
I strived to be the best me I could be
But sometimes that me just can't be set free

I think it's best for you to be free
Of my nightmares, of my daydreams
Even if you see me in your sleep
You'll find that things are not so steep
You'll have white nights and bright days
You'll never walk astray
You won't lose yet another day

You'll never have to see me cry
It might come as a surprise
But you'll start to feel like you float
Your boat will be much more stable
Without the force that disables

Don't try to argue back
'Cause I'm already packed
Just let me take you in
For one last time
I know I'm not allowed to win
But just this time
Let me stare a little while
before I say goodbye

ABOUT TO RAIN

I think it's about to rain
Should I get on that train?
I can't stop this train of thought
It feels like my head's about to pop

Knives and razors cut thin lines
Across the skies of my mind
And even if I want to speed things up
I can't erase this slow motion; it's a trap

My feet are sinking in quick sand
I'm in need of a quick hand
But all I see is a barren field
The sun's making my skin peel

The sand's getting in my eyes
I think I'm about to cry
But my eyes are so dry
The desert's frying me alive

I try to take cover from the sun
But it looks like I'm the only one
No help is on the way
I feel like a stray

God, it really looks like it's about to rain
Maybe I'll just get on that train

SOMETHING THAT I CAN HOLD ON TO

I'm trying to find something that I can hold on to
I open the blinds and look through muddy windows
I stare at the ceiling; since when has that stain been there?
I take a look at the walls, they're all covered in mold
I finally face the door; its knob is colder than the hard marble floor

But there's some light coming in through the windows
And it's making me feel like some heat might start spreading
So I open the windows, but all I see is lanterns
Lanterns lighting the cold twilight
I thought there was still daylight; when did the sun start going down?

I'm thinking about heading back to my hometown
I think it might be fun; I might find something to hold on to
And I search through old drawers; I find ancient photos
They're so old that just a touch makes the paper crack
I can barely make out the faces and places amid this sea of spots both bright and black

And I find even older photos and letters and maps
As soon as my fingers brush against the surface, the paper turns to dust
And now there's dust everywhere; I don't feel like I can be here
Even the door's cold knob is starting to show its rust
If I don't bust out of here, I might become dust myself

And the dark is setting in; I really shouldn't be here

The lanterns' lights are starting to shrink
So I run; I run home; away from my hometown
Straight into the night sky
Amid these bright and dark spots, I guess maybe I'll find something I can hold on to

THE THING

I don't know what the thing is
Or where the thing is
I wish I could find something to say
A way to make this all go away

I try to keep my eyes open
But they might as well be closed
I'm feeling down and broken
It's like I'm glued to the floor

I think I see a door
But it's so high above
I will never reach it
I don't even know why
But I try to reach it

But I'm still glued to the floor
Is there anything more?
I'm always about to explode
I can't take this anymore

I wish there was a way to tell you
I wish there was a way to show you
I wish I could skip the silence
I wish I could pause the blockage

Would the walls finally fall?
What would have been the toll for this all?
Would I at least be able to crawl?
Would we get to the other side of the wall?

YESTERDAY'S SPECIAL

I thought I was here for a reason
It seems like I'm the cause of my own treason
I try to reason with myself
But it's like trying to draw water from an empty well

I thought I saw myself walking, standing, running
Now I really can't tell if it was just my mind's shadow
I try so hard to disappear in the shadows
To dive into corners and free fall while I'm standing

But no matter how thick the dark gets
I always hear the clock tick
And the sunlight makes me trip
The rays rip right through me without regrets

I wonder what I'm gonna get today
Will it be yesterday's special?
Would that change if I try really hard?
I don't think there's anything special about yesterday

But I get the short end of the stick
I'm starting to feel sick
As yesterday finds its way into today
I wonder what I'm gonna get the day after today

SHADOWS

A million stars embrace me
Their light is so bright, so blinding, so hot
I'm floating in a sea of lights and shadows
This relief is concerning; the abysmal distance is alarming

I try to hit the brakes and touch the ground
But dumbfounded I find that makes me sore even higher
Now the stars seem too close, too bright, too blinding, too hot
I try to untie the knots that bind me to this vessel

I can barely see or hear anymore
The knots become undone, and I quickly hit the floor
And the floor is so dark, so dim, so cold
I'm crawling on a plane of ice and shadows
My need for relief is concerning; the lack of distance is alarming

SPACES

All I see is empty spaces
That are staring back at me in awe
They don't understand how I'm still here
When they've been there for so long

I look at their dark faces
Their bright faces
Their sad faces
Their smiling faces

They look at me with wide eyes
Warm eyes
Cold eyes
Until they shut their eyes

But my eyes are wide open
Waiting for the door to open
Waiting for the spaces to embrace me
Until I shut my eyes

Eyes shut and empty noises
Because there are no voices
I race to each space looking for answers
But often times spaces are like mazes
Neither empty nor full
Filled with secrets and haze
Just waiting for you to trip like a fool

I guess I'll wander blindly forever around these empty spaces
While I wonder if they'll ever reveal an answer

Eyes shut and ears shut
Because their only answer is that there won't be any answer

A CHANCE

I know you're not from around
I can see you like to take your time
You'd love to just sit there for a while
To close your eyes and let the water rise

You'd wait all day on your own if you could
I guess if I were you, I would too
If my feet were blistered and my bones crushed
I'd also want to stay on the ground, lips hushed

I'd look at faces and eyes only finding lies
I'd look at streams in the skies, no sunrise
I'd be screaming inside and hiding outside
But I can't see you like that; I can't lie

I can't lie; I can't be the one who opens your eyes
But I can me the voice that drowns out the noise
I can bring in some light to dispel the shadows
You think the water's too deep, but it's rather shallow

Don't turn around; don't shut your eyes
Look at my voice; let it fill the voids
Dip your feet in my eyes' ponds
Let the warm water wash over you so you can respond

I won't let you fall; I swear
I know you hear more than just words
Would you give me a chance?
Would you take my hand?

PUPILS

I wonder what your eyes think when they look at me
I wonder what they'd both say if they knew the truth
Would they agree with me? Would they look the other way?
Would they stand in each other's way? Would you let them play?
With your right eye looking right and your left eye looking left
Would you be deaf to my words? Would you blow up in silences and leave sound in debt?

That would sound like a theft to me, like you're stealing my brightest colors
And then leaving me only with my darkest shadows
I jump into my pupils and dive to the depths, but all I see is shadows
It's the deepest, darkest, thickest black you'll find; a thousand circles devoid of color
My kicking feet are causing ripples in the dark; I think I'm swimming upwards
But I'm actually starting to drown; the black water goes into my throat and drips downwards

A thin, raw gasp comes out of my mouth as I try to grasp something
Something; give me something; say something; do something
My eyes are covered in a black veil; the stickiness is plugging my ears
Echoes? Echoes... Voices? Voices... Soft voices; sweet voices; tender hands
They try to grasp something while they say something
They shake me and pluck me out of the dark seas in my eyes

And your eyes shine with light; they're not looking left or right
They've both agreed that they want to be looking at me

PLANET

I saw you from afar
Your face hidden behind my scars
I thought you were just passing by
I didn't even plan to try

And my foot was already on the doorstep
I was so afraid of falling without being caught
But the echoes of your voice wrapped themselves around my feet
Like soft threads they pulled me back and twisted my thoughts

I still thought I wouldn't be able to make it
My mind was bending and breaking
But whenever I tried to run away
I always ended up staring at your face

And your face got closer each time
Your eyes still hid behind my scars
But I was finally starting to see some stars
Stars both big and small that started to tare holes in the dark sky

"I'm just passing by"
My scars whispered these words into my ears
While they covered and blinded my eyes with layers of fear
But the soft weight of your threads made me want to try

I tried and tried; I twisted and bent
I even cried at times; I had to count to ten
I tried and cried and breathed and bent
Until I got there; a step closer to your face

And your face and my face

And the stars in your eyes
Put some rain in my gaze
That could wash out a maze

I bet these drops could also make plants grow
In this lonely new planet
Until it's lonesome no more
I hope I won't have to let the stars go
Because how can a planet be a planet
Without the warm glow from the stars?

MIS PASOS

Una cara entre un millón de caras. Un rostro sobre otro rostro. El tiempo que soba mi ventana. El viento que atraviesa las persianas. Un día como cualquier otro. Tan bueno como ninguno y tan malo como el otro. Y el tiempo sigue sobando mi ventana. Con cuántas ganas se asoma el tiempo compitiendo con el viento que insiste en acariciar las persianas de mi ventana.

Despierto cuando el mundo duerme. Me levanto cuando el sol calienta. El retumbo de mis pasos sigue el rumbo del ocaso. Dos millones de zapatos sobre mis pies hacen que todo gire al revés. Giran las agujas, desaparecen las luces y crecen las sombras. La penumbra me alumbra. La oscuridad me arrulla en su nido haciendo un hogar improvisado, tonto y desolado. Pero la oscuridad con su filo me corta. La extrañeza se me sube a la cabeza. No hay hogar en la sombra ni sombra de un hogar.

¿QUIÉNES SOMOS?

¿Quiénes somos?
¿Somos dos sombras huyendo de la luz?
¿O somos un alud de luz que destruye la sombra?
¿Somos la espada que penetra y corta todo a su paso?
¿O somos el espacio vacío que le impide el corte a la espada a su paso?
¿Somos el camino que se abre bajo la noche y la luz de la luna?
¿O somos la luna que por más que quiera nunca será fuego como el sol?
¿Somos el fuego que calienta, que sana, que abraza?
¿O somos las brasas que quedan después de que el fuego calienta y enfría?
¿Somos el frio que refresca después de deambular bajo el sol del desierto?
¿O somos el desierto que al anochecer congela con su frio?
¿Quiénes somos?

PIERDO MI ALIENTO

Como un suspiro en el viento
Como un grano de arena en la brisa
Así pierdo mi aliento
Sin pausa, pero sin prisa

Mis pensamientos se enredan
Creando obstáculos en la vereda
Tropiezo y me acerco al llanto, pero me levanto
Todo parece un espanto, pero aun aguanto

Aunque aguanto, no avanzo tanto
Las piedras en el camino me cortan el paso
Parece que se acerca el ocaso
Pero las rocas camuflan el sonido del lamento

Cuánto lamento todo este cuento
Toda esta historia marcada en mi memoria
Que al son de bucles que giran en silencio
Se repite en el tiempo dejándome sin sustento

Y cuando me sostengo, me deslizo
Si me deslizo, me vuelvo a sostener
Respiro en una cuerda floja, ¿quién me puede detener?
Pero, aunque tense y afloje, mantengo la distancia con el piso

Miro al piso, miro al techo
Que se sienta sobre mi pecho
Y así pierdo el aliento
Con un suspiro que sopla un grano
Que se monta en una brisa

Que se lleva el viento
Sin pausa, pero sin prisa
Moviéndose lento, flotando en el tiempo

COLGANDO EN EL VIENTO

Mi pelo colgando en el viento
Me recordó a tu movimiento
El canto de tu llanto retumbaba dentro
Venía lento, pero se acercaba el momento

Al verte no pude entenderte
El eje perdía su simetría
Mi expresión se vaciaba de simpatía
¿Cómo podría querer tenerte?

Te escuchaba mientras tu voz se gastaba
Tu luz se apagaba y te quebrabas
Y a tu paso quebrabas todo a tu alrededor
Ese era tu temor, que sólo ese fuera tu valor

Y tuve que estar de acuerdo
Sólo ese era tu valor
Me miraste con horror
Al ver que este no era tu puerto

Como un marinero errante te fuiste en tu velero
Con tu nave oxidada y tu vela rasgada
Lo cierto es que tu destino era incierto
Tu última llegada sería la anterior a esta salida

Casi celebraba tu partida
Cuando de repente se abrió una herida
Tu pelo colgando en el viento

Me recordaba a mi movimiento

LASTRE

Me disparaste
Me equiparaste a un desastre
¿Acaso sólo soy un lastre?
Un lastre que te arrastra
Hasta que dices "¡Ya basta!"

No tengo palabras para explicar
Lo difícil que es integrar tu mirar
Me persiguen los faros en tus ojos
No lo corrijo; son mi prefijo y sufijo

Y trato de escapar de este castillo de arena
Salto y corro; es una faena
El cielo truena; se acerca una tormenta
Respiro y paro; cuento hasta cincuenta

Cien, doscientas, trescientas veces te lo repetí
Y nunca me miraste, sólo me disparaste
Los agujeros atraviesan mi piel
El humo carcome mis ojos como hiel

Las gruesas gotas de lluvia mojan la arena
Pero se sienten como ácido en mi cara
Escuché que lloverá hasta la vida eterna
Más que un milagro me pareció una cosa rara

Pero así fue
Y de golpe el castillo se derrumbó
Entre los granos mi cara se hundió
Y sin más, entendí el desastre de ser un lastre

INVISIBLE

No sé qué pasa cuando llueve
Me pregunto dónde está toda la gente
El silencio llena todos los espacios
Que las gotas dejan cuando se mueven despacio

El sol se desapareció de golpe
Ahora las sombras cubren cada esquina
Sin pensarlo me termino sintiendo torpe
¿Cómo es posible que mi sombra sea tan fina?

Si con cada paso me roza un balazo
Y con cada suspiro me atraviesa un tiro
Pareciera que alguien sigue de cerca mis pasos
Me persigue y me lacera sin atrasos

A pesar de la discordia
Esta persecución se imprime en mi memoria
Si camino, tú caminas
Si me siento, te sientas conmigo

Tu obsesión conmigo
Me hizo creer que estaba siendo testigo
De que se alzaba mi valor, mi importancia
Miraba todo esto sin arrogancia

Pero hoy la lluvia que moja mis ojos
Va removiendo todos mis antojos
Y en un abrir y cerrar de ojos
No puedo evitar mi enojo

Mi vista se impacta al leer esta acta

El documento declara lo que dice tu mirada
No es sólo fina, sino que es invisible
Mi sombra es invisible

FANTASÍA

Ha pasado tanto tiempo
Me siento tan desconectada
Siento que no siento nada
Pero si recuerdo
Me traspasa una espada

Y nunca dijiste nada
Me tenías amarrada
Como el hada de tu cuento
Me tenías sin movimiento

Y cada encuentro me ilusionaba
Pensaba que nada nos frenaba
Pero siempre terminaba desilusionada
Al ver que el freno no se destrababa

Con trabas al mirar, trabas al hablar
Trabas al respirar
Me tragaban tus silencios
Me ahogaba en mis suspiros

Y así siguió esta fantasía
Soñando de noche con los días
Que nunca vería
Creando un derroche
De castillos en el cielo
Construyendo sin tope
Con barquillos con sabor a anhelo

Y nunca dijiste nada

Me tenías atrapada
Como al villano de esta pesadilla
Me dejaste sin ninguna vía

Expulsé mis silencios
Te ahogué en mis palabras
Destruí tu fantasía
Y la noche se convirtió en día

CORRER, CORTAR, ROMPER

La falta de certeza me corta esta cabeza
Esta cabeza que para bien o para mal siempre me acompaña
Esta cabeza marcada con voces de antaño
Donde corren rebaños de ovejas negras
Donde se disfrazan las brasas
Y sin atrasos atraen con sombras de frescor

No tengo valor para aguantar este calor
Sea frío, sea caliente, todo lo que quiero es temperatura ambiente
Pero este ambiente tóxico no me deja respirar
El aire es como resina epoxi
Me encierra en una caja hermética

Y casi pierdo mi ética cuando me ahoga el dolor
Me siento tan frenética, pero tengo valor
Se derrumba mi léxico, voy perdiendo el poder
Tal vez sea muy explícito, pero sólo quiero correr

Quiero correr y cortar y romper
Partir el aire, romper el encierro
Cortar la caja y liberar los rebaños
Me pregunto cuántos años soñaron con praderas aledañas
Que cada oveja deje su rebaño sin escuchar las voces del regaño
Y cuando todo esté vacío y no haya más que frío
No será perfecto, pero no será prisión

THANK YOU

Dear reader,

Thank you for having taken the time to go through these poems. Whoever you are, whatever your situation is, I hope that you could find some value in them.

I hope that you know now that you're not alone, that others can feel similar things to what you feel.

I hope that you could get a glimpse of how emotionally painful having mental health issues can be, and of how much of a mental torture it is.

I hope we can continue normalizing mental health together. If you didn't read the preface, it would be really great and helpful if you did.

Find me on Instagram as c.h.lakes so we can talk about it, because remember, mental illnesses are just as important and valid as physical ones. We have to start talking about mental health without shame, without being scared, without holding ourselves back from being raw about it.

Made in the USA
Middletown, DE
03 January 2023

21329622R00050